Dartmoor Letterboxes

ANNE SWINSCOW

KIRKFORD PUBLICATIONS

First Published March 1984
by Kirkford Publications
Cross Farm, Diptford, Totnes, Devon.

Reprinted August 1984
Reprinted March 1986
Revised June 1987
Reprinted May 1989
Reprinted April 1991
Reprinted July 1996

This book is dedicated to all those "Nut-cases" who spend their weekends, holidays, days off and any time they can scrounge; hunting for that most elusive object, the Dartmoor Letterbox.

Boxes come and boxes go, so there can be no definitive work on the subject. But I hope this may be of interest to those starting the hobby, and of amusement to those who have been at it for years.

Illustrations on page 9 and page 73, reproduced from old photographs, by Fiona Hughes.

All other photographs by Daro Montag.

Printed in Great Britain by BPC Wheatons Ltd, Exeter

ISBN 0 9509114 2 9

CONTENTS

ILLUSTRATIONS

INTRODUCTION

The phenomenon of "letterboxing" may be beyond the comprehension of many. Yet it is an indisputable fact that the number of boxes has grown from a single one to four hundred and fifty – even if it took over a hundred years to do so, and in the pursuit of these elusive little boxes many people have acquired a new appreciation of the beauties of Dartmoor.

Among the many letters we receive weekly, (mostly appeals for help to find boxes, or from those wishing to join the "100 Club",) this fact stands out. A gentleman from Yeovil finished his letter by saying, "...I love the moor, in all its moods, and to pick up a few boxes on my walks makes it even more interesting." The "Denbury Dawdlers", when applying for their 100 Club badges said "... we have met a lot of very friendly people in the last 18 months, and we have learnt so much about Dartmoor and its history...", they also requested that their badges be addressed to their 4 year old son who had been on all their walks with them since the age of 2¼ and who was watching every post for his well earned badge to arrive.

He is not the only young walker, another letter asked for three badges, "...for Christopher age 7, Rachael age 4 and myself..." These are by no means the youngest letterboxers though, one young lady of 4 months does her boxhunting from the comfort of her father's back, though her parents do admit that she sleeps through a lot of it!

Headmasters and scoutmasters are often writing for box information to make interesting walks for groups of youngsters. The headmaster from a school in East Devon says "... all the children in my class have become very keen letterbox hunters – we have been walking the moor a number of times, now joined by our Police Liaison Officer."

Letters come from schoolboys, one saying "At our school we are swapping information with each other". But this is not always the case, as a quote verbatim from another letter tells:–"but there is one problem, J...... will not swap his list so do you think I could have a photocopy of the yellow sheet you sent him then I could photocopy it myself and give one to all

1

the very keen letterbox hunters in my class. I realise that everything could be simplified by coming to your house and copying your information and I will do so one day, but until we can get a space in our action packed weekends I cannot do so."

There is no doubt that many make use of the letterboxes as an added attraction for the young on Dartmoor walks. A mother writes "... the children like the idea very much, and I hope it will encourage them to walk with my husband and myself more often...", a member of the Dartmoor Preservation Association who takes groups of youngsters on the moor about 10 times a year likes to include a couple of boxes on the walk as an added encouragement.

It is not only the young who appreciate the letter boxes though, a Lt. Cdr. says in his letter "... I was very surprised at the vast number, (of boxes) however, I do intend to make it a hobby to extend my weekend walking from my home in Plymouth." Another writer says ".. as a regular walker on the moors I'm sure that I would find pursuing the letterboxes an interesting reason for my walks." A writer from Sussex says "We spent Easter, and all the week after, looking for letterboxes, and had one of the best holidays we have had. We managed 25 stamps in all and are very proud of them."

A letter that perhaps expresses it best, starts by thanking for the help he has been given in "starting out on this fascinating and absorbing hobby.." and continues "Since last January I have realised what enjoyment can be had in finding these boxes, and looking for them in parts of the moor I would otherwise have only casually glanced at."

A cutting from a local paper informs us that the St. Anne's Chapel Women's Institute had a "...very interesting and amusing talk on 'The Letterboxes of Dartmoor'", and groups of handicapped adults are joining in the pastime by having boxes that are close to the road, brought to their ambulance so that they collect stamps on their outings. Letterboxing is for all!

The 100 Club badge is an added incentive to many, and one letter mentions "My little girl says she is going to award hers to her legs and sew it on her jeans!" But perhaps the most amusing place where the 100 Club found fame was in the 1983 Local Elections, where one candidate, setting out his claims towards being elected, states that he is "a member of the exclusive Dartmoor 100 Club." I don't know if this gained him any votes or not, but it did show how seriously some folks take things!

Just to prove that letterboxes are not as serious as all that, here is a series of poems, all concerned with the finding of one elusive box:–

There was a crooked man
Who walked a crooked mile
searching for a letterbox
That didn't make him smile.

He searched the moor all over
He thought it was a bore
He must have scoured a hundred rocks
And nearly every Tor.

He heard some bells a'ringing
A message they did tell
Look at the Tor over there
But the box is hidden well.

He ran across in a hurry
He was searching very fast
I'm really sure it must be here
For over there's the mast.

He searched and searched and searched,
But alas, he searched in vain
And there was nothing more to do
But come back, and try again!

As a clue, that really told one nothing, so we tried to gain further information.

We've searched Church Rock and Over Tor
And every inch of blasted moor
We though we'd solved your clues all right
But *still* there is no box in sight

With anagrams and cryptic clues
And poems full of useless news
We're sure we're hunting the right spot
Please tell us, are we getting hot?

The Diptford Hounds came out to sniff
We hoped that they would find it, if
There was a box there to be found
Or is it buried under ground?

We hope this box is not a fraud
Because we're getting rather bored.
So if there really is anything there
Please give us just a clue of – where?

The reply was a little more forthcoming, but kept up the poetic vein.

I was sad to hear of your weekend on the moor
Not finding the box on Over Tor
I'm grieved to know you're getting bored
But I promise that there is no fraud.

I thought the Diptford Hound would sniff it out
But perhaps a vet should see his snout
If as a boxhunter you wish to rank as best
Try searching clitter to the West!

Well, we eventually found it, after much searching, so wrote a poetic thank you letter.

Thank you for your latest clues
And letter bearing still more news.
On Friday, armed with wife and hound.
We went to see what could be found

And peering under every stone
We found vast quantities of bone
And coco-cola tins galore
And sandwich wrappers by the score.

J.B. who came too, brought a stick
And poked it into every nick
And cranny under all the rocks,
We all bent double like old crocks.

With several heads and lots of clues
We pooled our knowledge and our views
Until by luck – more than our skill
A plastic bag produced the "kill".

So now our names are in the book
You'll find them if you take a look
The hound has stamped her paw in ink
And left a smudge there in pale pink.

There seems to be something about letterbox hunting which inspires one to verse, but Sylvia Tancock (or "Jane Stewer") can express herself with style – and has put in verse what every letterbox would like to say:–

I am a Dartmoor letterbox.
I'm stuck up on the moor.
This is a most benighted spot,
Well hidden, that's for sure.
I used to have a lovely home,
A dry and sheltered place;
But then my owner sent me on
The transitory race.
Now hardly anybody comes
To visit through the week;
But Saturdays and Sundays, well,
They all play hide and seek!
The walkers come up in their droves
With compass, map and pen
Reciting clues in sing-song chant
To search me out again.
They trample down the heather bloom.
The stones toss left and right.
They flatten all the grass and worts
And leave a messy sight.
They scribble in my once clean book,

Exposing it to damp.
They scrabble for the inky pad,
All eager for my stamp.
If any other walker comes
And sees them, they will cry
"Get out you interloper, go!
You are a rotten spy!"
Though some of them are friendly chaps,
A clue or stamp will swap
While passing on the messages
And talking endless 'shop'.
And what a funny lot they are –
They 'plod' or 'hop', and then
"The hand of man hath never trod'?
And as for that there Ben....
Does Godfrey ever stay at home?
Who writes the latin lore?
Who stays to cook the fish and chips?
Or mind the Ramblers' store?
Now on a dark and stormy night
When tucked up cosily,
Remember poor unfortunates
Left on the moor, like me.
For through the rain and wind and snow
We huddle, from the shocks,
Your pleasure to provide, someday,
Your friendly Letterbox!

All this may be Greek to those who are new to Dartmoor
letterboxes, so enough of commendations and poems and let
us start at the beginning.

Chapter 1

When we talk of letterboxes on Dartmoor, we conjure up a very false picture. One's mind imagines a cast iron, red painted box, standing in the middle of some barren spot; where one can post a letter to one's nearest and dearest. This duly being collected by an enterprising member of the G.P.O. staff in his little red van, sorted, franked and eventually delivered to its recipient.

Far from this urban and up to date visage, the first of the Dartmoor letterboxes was merely a bottle stuck in a bank. This was placed at Cranmere Pool in 1854. At this time Cranmere Pool was an exceedingly inaccessible spot, and the Victorian gentlemen (and occasional lady) who braved the miles of bog-hopping it entailed to reach the Pool, were justifiably proud of their achievement, and recorded the fact by leaving their calling-card in the bottle.

By 1888, when William Crossing wrote of an excursion to Cranmere, the bottle had obviously been replaced, and the pattern of the modern letterbox was set. In his "Amid Devonia's Alps", he writes... "In the pool is a little heap of stones, and in a hollow in this is kept a small tin box – I have seen two there – for the reception of the cards of visitors. The spirit of vandalism, unfortunately but too prevalent, may have intruded itself here, but on the whole, the contents of the boxes seem to be respected. I can at all events affirm that I have found names there – my own among others – which had been left at the Pool several years before."

The spirit of vandalism is obviously not a product of the Twentieth Century, but in spite of vandals, ghosts and the elements of nature, the letterbox survived, and in April 1905, two keen moorland ramblers placed a visitors book in the box. In the first nine months this attracted 609 signatures, in 1906 there were 962 signatures, in 1907, 1,352 signatures and in 1908, 1,741 signatures. Although the greater majority of visitors called on the box in summer, this still shows how keen walkers were to reach this spot and sign the book. It must be remembered that this was in the days before the construction of the military road, and the shortest route to Cranmere was 7½ miles. Not 7½ miles of easy walking either, but a series of ups and downs interspersed by sections of bog-hopping. The easier route of 9 miles, via Walkham Head was perhaps the more suitable one for ladies, when one considers the dress of the time.

The name "Cranmere Pool" is rather misleading, as it could neither be called a mere, or a pool in its present state, but rather a depression within a large and somewhat barren area of peat, the last reference to it actually containing any depth of water, was when the Reverend E.A. Bray visited it in 1802, and remarked that the water could not be any more than 6 or 8 feet deep when it was full.

There are many stories and theories as to why it was emptied in the first place. The two most likely ones being that the bank was breached by local sheep farmers who had had sheep drowned in the pool, and so let the water out to prevent further losses. Or that during a very dry summer the bank was cut so that the water could flow in to the West Ockment, to supplement the supply for a mill near Okehampton.

Other people connect the emptiness of the pool with "Bengie", or Benjamin Gayer, one time mayor of Okehampton, who, for his misdeeds was condemned to empty out the pool with a sieve. A hopeless task, till he found by chance the carcase of a sheep, and after he covered the sieve with the skin, he was able to empty the pool. Bengie, or Bingie, is still said to haunt the area of Cranmere, having now taken on the form of a black colt. But while the Dartmoor ponies mostly avoid the area, it is more likely to be from natural caution of the boggy ground than from fear of the supernatural.

The most famous person to sign the visitor's book at Cranmere, was the late Duke of Windsor, who, as Prince of Wales, was guided there by J. Endacott on the 19th of May 1921.

....In 1905, a visitors book was placed in the box...

In 1894, a second letterbox appeared on Dartmoor, at Belstone Tor. This box has always carried an air of mystery. The original box was said to contain:- a visitor's book, newspaper cuttings and a bag of coins, but as anyone who found it was under promise to keep its position secret, there has always been some doubt as to its original site.

In the early 1940's a box was discovered at Taw Marsh, by a Mr. Pike, but he kept its whereabouts a secret till the Water Board started to build a weir in the vicinity, and the box was then removed for safety. It was returned to the grand-daughter of the founder of the original box, who wished to keep it. But – were Taw Marsh and Belstone the same box, under different names, or had there at some time been two boxes? Maybe the Belstone box had at some time been re-sited at neighbouring Taw Marsh. The whole truth will probably never be known; but as there is now a box at Taw Marsh, and another at Belstone Tor, honour is satisfied on all accounts!

The box on Belstone Tor maintains the tradition that all those who find it keep its whereabouts secret. The stamp is changed each September, every stamp having a new design. The first of the new stamps, put out in September 1978, was worded:– BELSTONE TOR, NORTH DARTMOOR, ESTABLISHED 1978, but whether this or Taw Marsh replaces the original box is a moot point.

The 1978 visitor's book records the gratitude of the many letterbox hunters who had previously spent many hours searching for a (probably) non-existent box. Two Box-hunters, signing themselves "Exeter Boghoppers" were even moved to verse, and wrote the following:

Yer us be again on Belstone Tor
Us have looked under stones by the score.
Up and down and around this stony tor
Us have spent fifteen hours or more.
A little help us surely needed
From a local gent, who had succeeded.
At LAST! Us found this yer Belstone box
Down yer among these gert big rocks.

Belstone Tor from the west, home of the Belstone Box.

Not strictly poetry, nor apparently strictly sticking to the rule of no one revealing the box's whereabouts. But heartfelt all the same!

In 1938 a box was placed at Duck's Pool, in the centre of the South Moor. Like Cranmere Pool, Duck's Pool is a misnomer – there are no ducks, and no pool. The site is just a boggy hollow near the head of the Plym. Perhaps at one time there may have existed a pool there, but if so it was probably drained by the tin miners many, many years ago; there is much evidence of their old workings in the neighbourhood.

The Duck's Pool box was set up in memory of William Crossing, the great Dartmoor writer and gazetteer. His book, "Crossing's Guide to Dartmoor", first published by the Western Morning News in 1909, has been constantly re-printed, and is still one of the most comprehensive guides to Dartmoor, in spite of the changes in the landscape that have taken place since his day. The fact that he wrote of a great number of places not even shown on the current 1:25,000 maps, makes his guide an invaluable help to any serious letterbox hunter.

The Duck's Pool box was financed by a group of Plymouth walkers known as "Dobson's Moormen", who under the instigation of Mr. J. W. Mallim, raised funds to pay for a stamp, a book and a plaque to the memory of William Crossing. This memorial, and the stone built box at Cranmere Pool are the only outward signs of the hundreds of letterboxes scattered over Dartmoor. One or two others were cemented in, in the early days, but these have been removed and re-sited where they can cause no offence to land-owner or beauty lover. Cranmere pool remains because it was the "daddy" of all Dartmoor letterboxes, and Duck's Pool stays as a permanent reminder of a great Dartmoor man.

The number of letterboxes progressed slowly, till, in 1976 Mr. Tom Gant produced a souvenir guide map to the 15 letterboxes in existence at that time. This excellent little publication not only had the effect of encouraging people to walk on Dartmoor and enjoy its beauties, but also produced a host of letterboxers!

The Ducks Pool Box, set up in memory of William Crossing.

Chapter 2

The next batch of letterboxes were, on the whole, well sited and professionally made. Many of them were put out by organized groups, such as scouts, schools, university students, the Junior Leaders Regiment, etc., and those who put out a box undertook to maintain it.

This tradition was continued through most of 1977, then gradually individuals put out their own personal box. Usually an ammunition tin, or a plastic container such as an ice-cream box, each containing a visitor's book, stamp and ink-pad. The stamps varied from well drawn symbols of the site, such as a fox for Fox Tor, or a cuckoo for Cuckoo Rock, to simple designs of wording only.

Towards the end of the year, home made stamps started to appear, at first not always very successful. A few people attempted lino-cuts. While there was nothing wrong with the designs, and they probably printed out quite satisfactorily at home on the kitchen table, they proved useless for the moors. For one thing, to print a lino-cut well, you need a flat surface – a thing Dartmoor does not abound in. Whereas most serious letterboxers now carry their own ink-pad and a piece of flat board, to be sure of getting a good impression, few letterboxers were so dedicated in the early days. Lino-cuts also entail inking up a roller, a refinement which can prove difficult while trying to balance a block on your knee in the pouring rain!

Next came home-cut rubbers. At first these were a bit primitive and experimental. One of the earliest, a cheeky little bird of unknown species, had a note in the visitor's book telling you to ink in the eye for yourself. Since those days rubber cutting has progressed to a such a fine art, that many home-made stamps are highly elaborate and almost indistinguishable from the professionally made, though a few still leave much to be desired. It is an odd fact that whereas home-made stamps are cut from rubber, many professional "rubber" stamps are now moulded in clear plastic.

With the spate of new letterboxes came unforeseen problems. Many of them were put out by those who had previously had no interest in Dartmoor, and with no respect for property or antiquities. As the number of Tors without a letterbox on dwindled, some were sited at stone rows, cists and ancient ruins. Though this in itself was not a bad thing, as it brought to the attention of the uneducated or the uninterested some of the objects of great interest on Dartmoor that they would otherwise never have heard of or visited, it unfortunately brought danger to the objects themselves.

Boxes were becoming better hidden as they grew in number, and a few people were almost prepared to remove a burial cairn stone by stone if they could not find a box they knew to be hidden there. Another box-owner, hid his box between the rocks at the top of a large Tor, then he (or someone else) painted in large red letters on the rock; "LETTER BOX", with an equally large red arrow to show you which way to look.

It was hardly surprising that the Dartmoor Park Authorities took exception to what was going on, and in October 1977 an article appeared in the Western Morning News, entitled:– "War on Little Boxes littering Dartmoor". In this article they talked of a "rash" of boxes, and said that there were now 32 known ones on the moor, they agreed that Cranmere Pool, and perhaps one or two of the others, were special, but that all the new ones must go.

By October 27th, the letterboxers were replying, and in the Western Morning News of that date a spate of letters were printed. Under the title "Don't Destroy Letterboxes say Moorwalkers", letters were headed – "One good use"

– "Harmless Hobby" – "Real Challenge" and "only a Beginning", and one walker even produced an excellent cartoon, captioned – "VE HAF WAYS OF MAKING YOU WALK".

Throughout November the letters continued, but by the 17th of December an article was printed, headed "Cut Back in Dartmoor Letter Boxes to be Less Severe". The main reason for this change of heart had been a meeting in Exeter between walkers and the Park Authority, where, after a "code of conduct" had been drawn up, the authorities agreed that the boxes provided a challenge for hikers, and an incentive to get people walking on the Moor.

The code of conduct drawn up at the time, and still in use today, though never officially circulated, is as follows.

Boxes should not be sited:-

1. In any kind of Antiquity, in or near Stonerows or Circles, Cists or Cairns, or in any kind of Buildings, Walls or Ruins, Peatcutters' or Tinners' Huts etc.

2. In any potentially dangerous situations where injuries could be caused.

3. As a fixture. Cement or any other building material not to be used.

It was also agreed that boxhunters should assist in the monitoring of surface wear and tear, and the clearing of litter.

If someone new to the game, sport or occupation of letterbox hunting should inadvertently put out a box in an "out of bounds" position, they are likely to be asked to move their box. Nearly everyone who puts out a box, leaves their name and address in the front of the visitors book, so it is an easy matter to explain to them why their box should move. In fact with several hundred boxes currently on the moor, most newcomers consult one of the "regulars" as to where there is a boxless space. Otherwise, with boxes being so well hidden it is quite likely that you may find you have sited your box within a few yards of someone else's

As the average letterbox is quite small, perhaps about 8" by 10" by 5", they are easy to hide, and sometimes very hard to find in the vastness of Dartmoor. Anyone who has spent the afternoon searching half an acre of clitter for an object of this

....the average letterbox is quite small....

size will know what I mean! Especially as the box will almost certainly not be visible, but will be behind a loose stone or under a bunch of heather, easy to find if some kind soul has given you minute directions – but tricky otherwise.

While boxes were becoming more numerous all the while, they were also being better sited and better hidden, so the publicity died down. To the best of my knowledge there was no mention of them in the Western Morning News till October 1979, when they again got a mention in the letter page. In the letter of reply on November 10th., the writer stated;- "I regard these boxes as a silly fad which, like skateboards and skin tight jeans, will go away only to give place to something even sillier". Well, he was right about the skateboards, if not the letterboxes.

He did, however, go on to say that it was possible to find some virtue in the craze, as it resulted in getting people out on the Moor and actually doing something instead of sitting glued to a television set!

After this, local publicity stayed quiet for a bit, though an article on private caches in general, which included several examples of Dartmoor stamps, appeared in Stamp Monthly, and an article on the Dartmoor Letterboxes was featured in Great Outdoors of August 1980.

Chapter 3

THERE is reasoning behind calling a cache with a rubber stamp in, a "letterbox". This dates back from the early days when the box replaced the bottle at Cranmere Pool. It then became fashionable to not only leave ones calling card in the box, but also to leave a postcard, addressed to oneself, and duly stamped with a ha'penny stamp. As the box was fairly inaccessible, it was exciting to see when, and from where, the next visitor to the box came. The tradition being that the visitor who posted on your card, did not simply drop it into the Okehampton Pillarbox, but should post it back to you from his home town. One always hoped that ones card would be returned bearing some exotic postmark.

This tradition is still carried on, though not to such a degree. As it is now quite usual to visit six or more boxes in an afternoon, and as postage has gone up sixtyfold, it would prove an expensive pastime if one left a card in every box. But it is still interesting to leave a card in one of the lesser visited boxes, as a way of finding out when the box next has a visitation. If one leaves a card in one of the better known boxes in the holiday season, one may be lucky enough to get it posted back by a Dutch or German visitor, though I must confess that if you do the postmark will more likely be Plymouth or Torbay.

As boxes proliferated, another aspect was introduced to the game. With the demise of the calling card, and the introduction of the visitor's book, people started looking for something more personalised than just their name written in the book. So began the advent of the "personal stamp". Like the box stamps these vary enormously in quality, ranging from the well drawn out design, professionally printed, to simple rubber-cuts, with perhaps toy printing set lettering. Most people give themselves semi-descriptive nom-de-plumes, though some seem obscure except to their owners.

As a guide, here are some of the hundreds of names that have appeared in the visitors books to date:–

"Followers of Felix", this one has a charming picture of a cat, presumably Felix who kept on walking.

"The Weary Wanderers", from Kernow, a stamp that speaks for itself.

"The Sniffers", with a lovely picture of a bloodhound, another self explanatory stamp.

"The Rainbow Enders", which sounds as if they are always searching for the crock of gold (or letterbox?) at the rainbow's end.

"Rattery Peat Pounder", with a weary walker pictured sitting on a rock.

"Diptford Letterbox Hound", my husband's personal stamp, has a picture of Mouse, our Yorkshire Terrier, who joins in boxhunting expeditions as often as she is allowed.

"The Moorons", a nice pun, especially as they are not lacking in brains.

"Hikaholics", the picture on the stamp being a half filled (or half empty) tankard of beer, with boots on.

"The Tortoises", one assumes are slow but steady walkers.

"The Tormentors" whose stamp also says:– "Seek and ye Shall Find", and has a picture of two little men who look prepared to dig up the whole moor if necessary.

"Roomtrad", which is simply Dartmoor in reverse.

"Jude the Obscure", so obscure, no one knows the reasoning behind that one.

There are hundreds of others, far too numerous to mention all. The Mudlarks, The Brixham Grasshoppers, and rival Grasshoppers from Paignton. The Dartmoor Prowler. The Pixyled Perambulators. Dartmorian. The Exeter Boghopper, and the Okehampton Boghoppers. Tormite. The Toruz and the Moortreckers are just a few of the more self explicit. Among the less easily explained, are: Sheep-scab (surely one

A selection of the "personal" stamps used by letterboxhunters 1

to be avoided); an Isosceles triangle, with the words Anonymous Hedgepig Hunter on the outside and four "W"s on the inside; and an eight sided figure with "Where the Hand of Man Hath Never Trod", written round the eight sides.

Many walkers are only known to each other by the stamps they leave in the visitor's books, and often it is quite a surprise to meet the owner of a "nom-de-plume" in person.

Some years ago it was decided to hold a get-together for letterboxers on the day the clocks changed from British Summertime back to Greenwich Meantime for the winter. This was to be at the Forest Inn, Hexworthy, an establishment where walkers are always well catered for. As there is no official method of communication between boxhunters, a note was left in many of the visitor's books, and those who knew other boxhunters passed the word around. With this somewhat haphazard method of notification, no one knew how many were likely to be there, but a stamp was made so that those who came could record the occasion for their collection, and the Inn prepared for about sixty walkers to turn up. The evening was a resounding success, with 160 people there. It has since been repeated twice yearly, on every Sunday that the clocks go either forward or back, and each time over 200 walkers attend.

So, thanks to "Dartmorten", who organises the event, and thanks to the Forest Inn who house it, a great many walkers who would otherwise only have been names in a book to each other, have been able to meet and swap news of new boxes and stamps, and to make new walking friends.

A selection of the "personal" stamps used by letterboxhunters 2.

Chapter 4

There are endless variations on the "hunt the letterbox" theme. One of the earliest of these which unfortunately faded out, was the Pixies' Treasure Chest. In the visitors book at the Laughter Tor box, supposedly the place "Where pixies laugh and play", a note appeared, inviting those who wished to find the Pixies' Treasure Chest to leave their name and address in the book.

Godfrey, my husband, was the first to apply. He was told to leave his car in a certain car park, and go to a given spot. When he reached the place, hoping to find a box with a nice new stamp in it, all he found was a note telling him to go back to the car for further details. Tied to the car door was a bag containing a cotton frock and a hat, and more directions. He was instructed to put on the clothes, and follow a trail of clues through Bellever Forest, shouting "I believe in fairies and pixies" as he went.

As he had been given strict instructions to go alone, he had a certain amount of difficulty getting into the unaccustomed garb – to say nothing of causing a vast amount of amusement to the other users of the car park! However, having got this far in his search for a new and rather special stamp, he had no intentions of giving up, though he did come near to doing so when his dress got tangled up in a barbed wire fence. But he eventually reached the end of the trail – or trial – and got his stamp (we feel it ought to have been a medal).

Throughout the morning he had seen no one who could possibly have been in any way connected with the box, so in an effort to find out who had been responsible, (other than pixies,) we made a ceramic treasure chest with a pixie sitting on it. This was taken to the next meeting at the Forest Inn, and displayed with a notice beside it, saying that the owner of the Pixies' Treasure Chest could claim it at 10 p.m. precisely. By 9.50, a crowd had gathered round the chest, but no one ever claimed it. So the mystery remains unsolved, and we still have on our mantlepiece a ceramic pixie to remind Godfrey of his jaunt over Dartmoor, in drag.

A more common form of variation in boxhunting, is the moving box, or the moving stamp.

Examples of the moving stamps are the Cuckoo in the Nest, and the Dartmoor Pony. These do not have a box of their own, but travel, with their latest finder, to the next box on the route. The cuckoo is a much travelled bird, one has no knowledge of where he will turn up next as whoever finds him may be travelling North, South, East or West, and the only proof of his having been at a particular box, is his stamp in the visitors book. He flies all over the moor, and no one, except whoever is carrying him at that particular time knows which box he is off to next.

Most of the moving boxes work as variations on a theme. The first one to appear was the "most Elusive" box, which stayed, for two or three months at a time, in out of the way sites. This was followed by the "Dartmoor Wanderer", the "Island Series", "Ye Olde Dartmoor Cross", the "Mystery Hill Series", "Dartmoor Dwelling" and several others. Some of the moving boxes are still on the moor, (and still on the move), while others have finished their tour and gone.

Each time the Island box and the Mystery Falls moved to a new Island, or a new waterfall, the stamp was changed to illustrate the new site, and with the Mystery Hill series, the stamp remained the same in design, but the name of the hill was altered with each new site. When the Dartmoor Dwelling box is moved, the picture, of an ancient hut-circle type of house, stays on each stamp, but the name of the current dwelling is inserted; such as Dolly's Cot and Hillson's House. This box is always hidden some way from the dwelling illustrated, in order to comply with the "code of conduct".

The Dartmoor Tramp moved around the North and South

25

moor, with a new picture for each new position. But its moorland tour came to an abrupt end when the box was burnt up during swaling (or gorse burning) on Wild Bank Hill.

Another variation on the moving theme was introduced with the Dartmoor Industries Series. It is surprising how many industries are, or have been connected with Dartmoor, and the series is concentrating on mines and workings of the past. The box is still on the move at the time of writing, but it has been to tin mining areas, such as Watern Combe, Doe Tor Brook and White Pits at Taw Marsh; also to Granite Ripping sites at Blackaton Brook on Throwleigh Common. There are many other sites of industries on the moor, so if this box escapes the spring burning, it will probably keep moving for a long time yet.

Yet another variation on the theme was instigated a few years ago by Bob Matthew. This is the annual Ten Post Box Walk. This can be done in groups or singly, and there are several routes, to cater for all types of walkers. The shortest is an 8 mile route, and the longest – for the really keen – is 25 miles. All the routes have check-points at ten different letterboxes, some established ones, and some put out for the occasion, and at the finish each entrant gets a certificate saying how far they have walked.

Chapter 5

At about the time that the controversy about the letterboxes was going on in the Western Morning News, a new box was put out at Calveslake. This was yet another variation on the theme. In the front of the book, instead of the usual name and address of the box's owner, and perhaps some information about why the box had been sited in that particular position, there appeared the following:–

> The world of the "arts" is ever so vast,
> But poetry seems to be dying out fast.
> This book is intended, when walkers arrive,
> To house all their poems, and keep it alive.
> So please, fellow walkers, join in with the game,
> Don't just stamp your map and enter your name.
> Sit down on a rock, have a think, take your time,
> Write down your thoughts in Limerick, verse or a rhyme.
> What we will do with them all – Heaven knows,
> We might even publish a book full of prose.
> So, fellow walkers, we all thank you for,
> Joining in with the fun at the box on this Tor.

The first to write a poem in the book, was obviously the same person who had put the book out in the first place. The fact that he both changed the colour of his ink and altered his writing, could not disguise the style of the person who signed himself with the symbol "Where the hand of man hath never trod". This, and some of his other rhymes were among the best that appeared in the book.

His first one, dated October 9th 1977 went:–

I'm first in this book, Bleak House was the same,
I now, as requested, take part in the game.
We all can walk (and it's thanks to God)
Where the hand of man hath never trod.
From Hen Tor I came, to Yealm Head I go,
Then over the hill to the cist at Stone Row.
Down to Grant's Pot where I'll just sign my name
And up to Duck's Pool, where I'll enter the same.
I then, like the Abbots, will walk down the way
To the car – at the end of a glorious day.
The Box up at Belstone I'm missing, so pray,
If you know where it is, why the hell don't you say?
Taw Marshes I've got, that's easy to find
But keeping them secret is not very kind,
The boxes are put there for walkers to use
If you know where it is, will you give me some clues.
Somewhere on Higher Tor's all that I've got
So two weeks ago I went out to that spot.
I searched every stone without finding a thing
If you know where it is – please give me a ring.

The next batch of poetic efforts hardly came up to this standard, though most people did in fact try to keep up the spirit of the book, even if in somewhat terser style; and offerings such as the following were common:–

Can this be the final box out on the moor,
I bloody well hope so, 'cos my feet are sore.

To find this box took some little time,
With 5 more boxes I will have 29.

I've walked all the way from Jersey
And I'm illiterate too,
I can't think of a good rhyme
So I'll leave it all to you

and – It's me, back again,
I walked off with the ruddy pen!

A few people waxed really poetic, Dartmorian, on his sixty-seventh birthday, wrote the following in the book:–

28

"Give me the moor and the hollow,
Let me breathe the air of the sea.
Sing me a song of the swallow
That for joy he sings to me.
Give me a bush for a pillow
And the shade of an old oak tree,
Give me the stream by the willow
And the winding road ever free."

On October 23rd 1977, just after the first article against letterboxes appeared in the Western Morning News, a poem was written in the book, the last verse of which went:–

Now Mr. M..... tells us he will close down all the boxes
And leave the Wilds of Dartmoor to the buzzards and the foxes,
So the standing stones of Dartmoor can once more brood in peace –
On the day that he decides that "letterboxing" has to cease!

On October 30th "The hand of man..." paid his second visit to the box, and continued on the same theme.

I'm here again for the second time
all set to write down my thoughts in rhyme.
The topic today is the Dartmoor Committee (that tyranical group without mercy or pity).
Their move to ban letterboxes seems so insane I simply can't think what they hope they will gain.
No damage is done, there are *no* beaten tracks and genuine walkers will *not* walk in flocks.
Long distance walking is with us to stay, whether boxes remain or are taken away.
On behalf of us walkers, I ask the Committee to leave us our boxes and exhibit some pity.

His third visit produced a poem which enlarged on this theme, and ended:–

....We ask the Committee to save the traditions and take notice of letters and angry petitions.

29

Before the agreement with the Dartmoor Authorities in December of that year, one more note on the same subject was written in the book:–

> In all my years, I've had no fears
> Of walking all of Dartmoor.
> But now watch out –
> There's a committee about,
> Not anti fox-hunting,
> But – – box-hunting
> Let every walker beware!
> (There is no truth in the rumour that the Devon
> County Council have allocated £1 million to
> tarmac all "the paths between the Boxes" which
> have been carved out by the many thousand
> Dartmoor walkers.)

The last bit being an allusion to the talk of "beaten tracks" in the Western Morning News.

After the compromise was reached, poems on the subject ceased, and the next popular topic was the weather – not really to be wondered at as it was now the middle of winter. Days were short, the moors were wet and cold, and so were most of the walkers.

> We've walked this way for many a mile
> But our children are cold and no longer smile.
> So excuse us please, we haven't the time
> To say all we want in a nice little rhyme.

So went one ode from two stout hearted walkers, with their children aged 3 and 1, braving the moors at the end of November.

Others made pointed remarks (in verse) on the same theme:–

> I struggle over Tors and dales
> Through wind and rain and snow and gales.
> To find a box and leave a card,
> My God – I find the going hard.

To North Moor today I said to the boys
To Cranmere, and Kneeset and similar joys.
A call to Okehampton produced poor report –
"There's more snow on them hills than anyone thought".
So back to the South, such familiar ground,
And lo and behold – a "new" box we have found.
To find every one you must be really nifty
I've learned just today there are well over fifty.

Tiz true what you say about the Northern Moor
Twaz thick with snow, visibility poor!

I'm here with my brother, we two,
We arrived here at 9.22.
It's beginning to rain
Yesterday was the same,
and my brother and I are wet through.

We don't want to displease
But if we stay long, we will freeze.

The wintry conditions even affected "the Hand of Man".. at
least two of his many poems in the book showed this:–

The weather today is extremly cold,
or maybe its just that I'm getting old.
Which ever it is, my hands are like ice,
with my feet just the same, it is not very nice.
My toes I can't feel and there's ice in my ears,
my nose is quite numb and my eyes full of tears.
But my heart says it's great to be out here again,
though my mind says YOU FOOL – you must be insane!

Even more admitting that the weather could occasionally
affect even his walking was the terse verse:–

NO! Your eyes don't deceive you
It's me once again
No rhyme can I write, it's starting to rain!

Many people wrote about Richard, "the Hand of Man...",
some politely and some in not such polite terms when they

found themselves expected to spout verse. But perhaps the best was a four line poem, which described him in a nutshell, it went:–

Across the Moor there walks a bod
Where the hand of man hath never trod.
He doesn't stay in inn or hostel,
But comes up weekly from St. Austell.

Maybe some day all the poems will get published, (or at any rate the cleaner ones), but I must just include two more which seem to express the fun of the Calveslake box, and letterboxing in general.

Oo-ar oo-ar ay, tis a beautiful day,
We come to this Tor, didn' quite know what for.
So whilst in the sun, I've had me some fun,
Oi've taken me time and written this rhyme.
Oo-ar

And finally:–

Rubber stamps in letter boxes
Aching feet, and soggy soxes.

That says it all!

Chapter 6

The letterboxes are often used for other things than just to stamp post-cards, and leave ones name in the visitor's book. Many books carry messages from one walker to another – some helpful, some unprintable – tantalising fragments of new exciting looking, stamps appear, usually with the words "out soon" written across them, and messages such as "Have you got the new stamp at Taw Marsh yet?" send keen walkers scurrying off in a new direction.

Clues to new boxes are also sent by post to regular walkers. Not only are these often in heavily disguised writing, but the clues are often somewhat ambiguous and take a bit of working out. For example, "An epoch, with a fairy-tale connexity" – turned out to be a new box at Slipper Stones. Clues like this may not be grammatically correct, but half the fun is trying to work them out.

Having worked the clue out, one still has no idea where on the particular Tor or area the box is hidden, and unless one is possessed of endless time and patience, and a certain amount of good luck, one's chances of finding it are still slim. So one then has to work out from the writing, the post-mark, the area and similar clues, who the postcard came from. Then, telling them that you think you have solved the clues, try to get them to divulge the grid-reference or some other clue as to the more exact whereabouts of the box.

Cunning letterboxers usually have a bit of information about some other box they can offer in exchange, and more "swops" go on than in many conventional stamp clubs.

Some of the other clues that have arrived through the post, are as follows:–

"You'll have heard of me, I'm Sir Winston C.
There's a Yankee girl lives down from me,
She holds a secret I'm sure you've guessed,
I'll give you a clue, now work out the rest.
        (Don't look for a ringside seat.)"

"A letterbox on the moor that's me
To be found I want to be.
I stand on high, I stand on low,
To miss me would be a blow.
A bird is close, so make the most.
Find me and you're sure to boast."

"From the fruit large ones surely could grow,
Somewhere within an "Elephant" lies below.
After dark some say our magic begins to show;
From the Destroyer's mark, East you must go.
        –The rest is up to you!!!"

These examples show that to be a successful boxhunter one needs a nimble mind, a working knowledge of the Moor, a good set of maps and preferably a copy of "Crossing's Guide". Otherwise how could one guess where a dog named "jumbo" lies buried under an oak tree?
Or for a change from verse try this one:–

"My first is a small item secretly worn by a bride, my second part is at the end of black and is also red, my last is where a road has to hold its breath! solve the problem, and 23 paces at 155 degrees will be your goal."

Occasionally a box sits out on the moor, unvisited, for six months or more. The clues given have been too sparse or too obscure for it to have been found. But not all boxes are meant to be difficult to find, often precise details are given, by post or phone call, or the location is described in one of the visitors·

34

PUPERS HILL SOUTH DARTMOOR

LEAD ME FROM DEATH to LIFE, from FALSEHOOD to TRUTH

LEAD ME FROM DESPAIR to HOPE, from FEAR to TRUST

LEAD ME FROM HATE to LOVE, from WAR to PEACE

LET PEACE FILL OUR HEART OUR WORLD, OUR UNIVERSE

DARTMOOR
WILLSWORTHY RANGE
RL.   83

Great Mis Tor
Presented By
1ST Crawley BB
w·w·w

HOLNE
EST 1980
MOOR
H

Post
HEN TOR
DARTMOOR
Box

The Plume of Feathers
ICH DIEN
19   81
Royal Forest of Dartmoor

FISHLAKE POSTBOX
DARTMOOR
OCTOBER 1968 · FEBRUARY 1981

AVON HEAD
Established 1978
SOUTH DARTMOOR

1962
DUCK'S POOL
DARTMOOR NATIONAL PARK

Bel Tor

A few of the many and varied Dartmoor Letterbox Stamps (past and present) 1.

books. Also one may find a note in a visitors book informing one of a new stamp at an old and long established box.

When there were only a few boxes out, most collectors merely stamped their map. But as boxes proliferated, other methods of display had to be found – or most people's maps would have become unreadable!

Some people collect them in a book kept for the purpose, but probably the most popular method is to put each stamp on a separate postcard. Cards can then be kept together in a box, filed, or kept in a postcard album, I have even seen them stuck in rows as wallpaper. Now that the standard of the majority of stamps has improved so much, they look very decorative however displayed. The ink pads in the boxes vary in colour, and as many people now carry their own ink pad as well, there can be a vast selection of pictures and colours. One or two of the grander stamps are even printed in two or more colours, and in the case of the "Four Seasons", a composite stamp in four segments of a circle with the name underneath, the completed stamp is a five colour one, a decorative addition to any collection.

Chapter 7

Who puts out all the letterboxes?

The answer is that anyone can. Though not a regular letterboxer, I have put out one myself, though that was in the nature of a joke that misfired. At that particular time we had a keen box-hunter painting the outside of our house for us, and over a cup of coffee one day he said, "If only I could find a new box and be first in the visitors book, I would give you a day's free painting". That was an opportunity too good to be missed, so I planned to set one up.

There was no time to get a professional stamp made, nor am I clever enough to cut rubbers, so I enlisted the help of a friend. She had a bought stamp of a vase of flowers, so we pored over a map of Dartmoor, trying to find a site that would suit the stamp. A place called Blue Jug seemed the most appropriate, but it was rather in the middle of nowhere, so we doubted our ability to find the place ourselves, let alone expecting someone else finding the box on our directions. Nowhere else seemed really to fit the stamp, so in the end we opted for Honeybag Tor, which apart from the connection between flowers and honey, had the added attraction of being fairly close to the road, and not having a box on it already.

On the pretext of taking the dogs out for a run on the moors, we set off. Complete with an ice-cream carton containing the stamp, ink-pad, a visitors book with carefully typed inscription that gave no clue as to who had put out the box – but dedicating it to all who enjoyed the Dartmoor Flora –, and two new biros.

Honeybag Tor was a bit of a shock. An ideal place to hide a letterbox, it is a huge mass of enormous rocks. In fact you could hide almost anything there. But our problem was that we wanted it to be easily found by the right person, but not too easily found by anyone else.

Eventually we found a suitable site that could be easily described, and having hidden the box, we went home and sent off some carefully worded postcards. So as to allay suspicion, we had to send off several, we knew that information gets pooled and passed around, and had we sent one only to the person we wished to find the box, he might have smelt a rat! His and Godfrey's were posted the same day, and a few others sent out two days later, that gave them a head start.

Godfrey, who was of course in on the plan, professed great surprise at receiving his card, and as it was a fine day it was agreed that painting could wait for another day, while a bit of box-hunting took place. So, Godfrey having been given verbal directions how to find the box after a simulated hunt, they set off.

It was more than a simulated hunt – they did NOT find the box. Perhaps it was my directions at fault, Godfrey's inattention, or the sheer size of the Tor, but they came back without the stamp, and our hopes of a day's free painting began to fade. Next day they went off to have another try, this time I had drawn a map so that there could be no mistakes. They found the box all right, but unfortunately it had been found already, so they were not first in the book. A Dutch holiday-maker and his family had come upon it quite by chance, and as they had all signed in the book, our elaborate set up to get a day's free painting done came to naught! The box is still there though, and I provide it with a new stamp every year.

Most boxes are put out for much simpler reasons. The most usual being that their owners just enjoy letterboxing. Some are put out to commemorate a special event. There has been one put out to celebrate a 21st birthday, one to commemorate the Falklands Victory, several are in memory of people who have loved Dartmoor, and one was even put out where a

Honeybag Tor.... a huge mass of enormous rocks.

lovelorn letterboxer used to sit alone when his fiancée was away.

Not everyone wishes it to be known that they are the instigator of a certain box, and people have hidden behind all sorts of names.

Some of these were obvious aliases, such as "Vinegar Tom and the Morbids", who were responsible for a rash of new boxes. But it might surprise the Sticklepath Womens Institute – if such an Institute exists – that they are the supposed owners of a letterbox, and that anyone who finds the box in a state of disrepair, or needing a new book, is invited to contact them.

Rather more difficult to contact box-owners are the "Nigerian Pole Vaulting Team". They were supposedly responsible for putting out a letterbox, and are also reputed to have signed in at several others. Well, letterboxing has become very popular, and foreign visitors have often signed in the books, but somehow I doubt this one!

"Die Essiger Männer" (or the pickle man) adds a continental air to some of the boxes, but this one is not a foreign visitor, just a nom-de-plume. Similarly "Llamedos" is not a visitor from Wales or Greece, as might be thought, but merely a reversal of letters. While the "Copy Cat", who has put out several boxes, COULD come from Cheshire, as the address he gives in the books suggests, but more probably he is a Lewis Carrol fan.

Not everyone, of course, hides under an alias, and the majority of boxes have the name and address of the owner, with perhaps a dedication, or a potted history of the site written clearly in the front of the visitors book.

One box, out for a short time, contained an autograph book. This was signed by the friends of the landlord of the Plume of Feathers Inn at Princetown, and given to him at his wedding, as a thank-you for all his services to letterboxers, and to wish James and Linda every happiness for the future.

Chapter 8

Godfrey's first 100 stamps were collected as a collage but as the number of stamps grew and grew, so did his collection. Not all the stamps, of course, come from new boxes, many boxes change their stamps yearly. Some are changed to improve them, or, regrettably, because vandals have taken them, while others will put out a seasonable stamp in their box, such as a special Christmas stamp, or commemorating an event such as the Queen's Silver Jubilee. All this means a lot of stamps.

There are also a lot of boxes, and it was these facts that made us feel there should be some reward, or target to aim for. Thus was born the 100 Club. The idea has been kept very simple, we designed a cloth badge that could be stitched on to a jacket or rucksack, and anyone who has visited, and collected the stamps from 100 different letterboxes is entitled to wear one. The badge, in green and white, says Dartmoor Letterboxes 100 Club. Other than this the club does not exist, there are no meetings, no committee and no membership fee, just the cost of the badge. Oddly enough the badge has proved very popular, probably for the slight air of prestige it carries. The fact that there are over 700 sold just goes to prove how popular letterboxing has become.

Probably because of the 100 Club, Godfrey's name became known to the local press, and the Tavistock Times printed a two page article about letterboxes. In this article, he was referred to as "....unofficial president of a club that doesn't exist....". The name has stuck, and he even received letters addressed to him in this manner – what is more, they have arrived! I sometime think the G.P.O. must think that certain members of the Devon public are a bit potty, when one sees some of the postcards they have to deliver. Addressed to someone's "letterbox name" on the front, and the back covered with cryptic clues and odd stamps.

Only the other day a letter arrived addressed to:

Mr. Godfrey Swinscow, (sec. D'moor 100 Letterbox Club)
Cross Farm,
Diptford?
Dartmoor (Somewhere)
Devon.
If not at above address, please try Cross Farm, Drewsteignton.

Well the letter arrived next day, in spite of the fact that Diptford is some miles from Dartmoor. Full marks to the G.P.O. on that occasion, though they are not always as bright. By the next post we received a letter that had been languishing in Dartford, Kent for three days before finding its way to us.

The cause of a lot of the letters is a sentence from the article in the Tavistock Times, ".... another tradition is that people who set up new boxes tell Godfrey where they will be...." This was not a tradition up till then, but seems to be becoming more and more of one, and of course it works both ways. If he is always told of new boxes, then he is also the person to contact when one wants to find a particular box. So to keep pace with all the letters and phone calls, the kitchen now looks like a war-time "ops." room, with pin marked maps, box-files and albums. Though I must confess that several people have now gone one better, and have their box finding clues all computerised!

One thing leads to another, and articles on Dartmoor Letterboxes were printed the following month in the magazine Devon Life, and in the Geographical Magazine. Devon Life sent a photographer who walked with Godfrey (and Mouse) to the box at Cranmere Pool; but we knew nothing about the Geographical article till after it came out in

Dartmoor Letterbox Stamps. (2)

print. As it published our name and address, even down to the post code, this led to another influx of letters, from potential letterboxers from all over the country.

It was all these articles that led to Spotlight Southwest featuring Dartmoor letterboxes; and Mouse became a T.V. star! For the feature we hid a special letterbox close to the road, in an accessible part of the Moor, so that the cameraman would not have to haul his equipment too far. The producer wanted Mouse to show a keen interest in the box. So, to get the right effect, not only did the box contain the requisite stamp, ink pad and visitors book, but it also had a little store of chocolate drops in. These had the desired effect, and Mouse put her nose in the box as keenly as a truffle-hound after truffles. Later, there were close up shots of Mouse, standing on a tussock with her ears blowing in the wind, that were enough to make one small dog very bigheaded.

This was not the only box to have contained "goodies" though. There has been a "Reward" box which contained a £5 note for the first finder, boxes which have contained cans of beer, one containing a miniature bottle of whisky, and Honeybag box always contains a little pot of honey for the first finder of each new stamp. There was a beautifully made copper cross for the first finder of the Hand Hill box which is 20 paces from the smallest cross on Dartmoor. There was also a bottle of wine for the first person to complete the Perambulation series. So apart from bringing the enjoyment of exploring Dartmoor and collecting stamps, letterboxing can bring unexpected rewards!

.....the smallest cross on Dartmoor.

Chapter 9

Some people collect letterbox stamps because they enjoy walking on Dartmoor, and find that hunting for boxes takes them to places they might never otherwise have explored. Conversely, some people have found that letterboxing has given them an interest in the flora and fauna and historical aspects of the moor that they never had before. It is a fact that the majority of people who go to Dartrmoor never venture more than 100 yards from their cars, but the great interest shown in collecting stamps has introduced many people to the wider interest of the moor itself.

Dartmoor is a paradise for the pre-historian and the industrial archaeologist. It is hard to walk anywhere on the Southern Moor without coming across reminders of our Bronze Age ancestors, while at Corringdon Ball and Cuckoo Ball there the remains of Neolithic chambered tombs, proving that Dartmoor has been the home of man since the fourth millenium B.C. There have also been occasional finds of stone tools dating from this period, though no trace of any Neolithic settlement has yet been found actually on the moor, the area was at least used for hunting and summer grazing by these peoples.

By contrast, the area must have seemed relatively crowded in Bronze Age times. The moor offered most things that man needed. The climate of that time was rather warmer than today, and whereas the lowland areas were heavily forested, the moorland uplands offered large areas of safe grazing, with ample water for the animals. There was plenty of stone for housing, stone that needed no quarrying, but was scattered

....and one of the largest, Siward's Cross near Nuns' Cross Farm.

freely on the surface ready for use, peat for fuel, and in some areas, soil suitable for cultivation.

Remains of Bronze Age homes, (hut circles) are to be found scattered over the moors. As their name suggests, they were circular dwellings, the walls built of large, unworked, granite stones reinforced on the outside with smaller stones and turf. The roofs would have been of turf or heather, supported by rafters converging to a central post. The remains of charcoal and cooking stones found in excavated sites proves that they were built for human habitation, not as stores or animal shelters.

Whereas some hut circles are found singly, or in small groups, others were surrounded by a retaining wall. These enclosed settlements, or pounds as they are known, are usually roughly circular, and contain varying numbers of hut circles, and sometimes the remains of other buildings. These probably housed the cattle and sheep, which would have been driven into the pound at night to protect them from the wolves and bears which still inhabited Britain at that time. Although partly restored, Grimspound is a very good example of this type of settlement. Ryders Rings, though not so easy to see as a whole, is a very interesting example of a double enclosure, with hut circles inside the enclosures, and stock pens built along the inside of the retaining wall.

While keeping to the code of conduct, and not siting letterboxes too close to ancient remains, several boxes have been put out to highlight these moorland archaeological sites. There has been a box at Erme Pound, two overlooking Grimspound, two near Ryders Rings, and a box commemorating "Hut Circles of the Bronze Age" was sited below Kings Tor, which is an area containing many hut circles and small enclosures.

There are many other signs of habitation dating from around this time, stone rows, standing stones, stone circles and burial monuments. Some of which were barrows, but many were the unique Dartmoor Kist.

The kist – or kistvaen – was like a stone box sunk into the ground. The sides and ends were slabs of unworked stone, and there was a coverstone over the top. The earlier

LICH PATH

Dartmoor's Ancient Stone Rows

2 MERRIVALE AVENUE

EXETER ABOUT AROUND CLUB
Grimspound

Ernestorre · 1240 · FOREST PERAMBULATION

Forest of
Quintins
Man
Dartmoor

HUT CIRCLES OF THE BRONZEAGE
PREHISTORIC DARTMOOR

JUDE THE
The Abbots' Way
OBSCURE

Stamps of Dartmoor's Historical past.

specimens were large enough to have contained a body buried in a curled up position, but later examples were smaller, and were used for cremated remains, a fact which has been verified by traces of burnt bone having been identified in some of them. Though the acid soil of Dartmoor has destroyed all traces of other human remains.

Many of these kists were encircled by a ring of standing stones, which in most cases was the retaining wall for the mound of earth which would have covered the grave. Other kists have been found under cairns, and the cairns themselves would have been covered by earth and turf – forming a barrow. Though a good many barrows have been despoiled by the tin miners using the stones to build themselves huts with, there are still a good many examples to be seen on the heights of the south moor.

One of the best examples of a large kist is at the Merrivale sanctuary, but unfortunately the splendid coverstone has been split in half. Other large kists can be seen at Lakehead Hill, Roundy Park near Postbridge, and to the north east of Wild Tor. Smaller kists can be found in dozens of sites, many of them close to the road. A good example is at the edge of the Forestry Commission plantation on the by-road from Postbridge to Widecombe, and another at the foot of Hound Tor, to name just two. Most, though not all, are marked on the Ordnance Survey map, and for those interested in ancient history there is always something of interest to be seen when one is out on letterboxing expeditions. Burial sites that have been commemorated by stamps are Grims Grave, Giants Basin and King Barrow.

Houses for the living and houses for the dead are not the only ancient remains on the moor. A study of the map will show the numerous sites of stone rows, circles and standing stones. Whether or not the average boxhunter is interested in the Bronze Age, they cannot fail to be impressed by the sheer magnitude of some of these. The longest of the stone rows, from Stall Moor to Green Hill stretches for more than two miles and crosses two rivers, rising over 300 feet on the way. It is in fact, almost certainly, the longest prehistoric stone row in the world, and it starts and ends with a burial cairn. This row will have been seen by many boxhunters, as there has been a letterbox at each end, and also a box at Stingers Hill, marking "The Centre of Dartmoor's Longest Stone Row".

There are many other stone rows. Single rows, double rows, rows in pairs, treble rows, short rows and long rows. Their purpose is a mystery, though they are assumed to have a Religious/Astronomical significance, as are the equally numerous stone circles and standing stones, or menhirs. One of the tallest and most solitary menhirs, Beardown Man, had a letterbox to keep him company for many years, and the Dancers and Nine Maidens stone circles have both had letterboxes, though sited at a discreet distance. But however many letterboxes are put out by modern man on the moor, their number seems insignificant when compared to the remains of occupation left by ancient man.

Chapter 10

It is difficult to imagine what Dartmoor must have looked like before man began to industrialise the entire area. The pastoral farming communities, when they forsook their stone tools, needed bronze; and to make bronze they needed tin.

The first supplies of tin-stone were easily picked up from the river beds. After the stones were crushed and the ore extracted, it needed to be smelted; and so the industry, which was to be carried on on the moors for centuries, was begun. As the supplies of easily picked up tin-stone dwindled, so the moor began to be dug up and turned over, rivers and streams changed their courses as they were dug into, and spoil heaps were left along the banks.

Smelting required great heat, so the plentiful peat banks were dug to make charcoal. As man's knowledge progressed, so did his needs, and as well as digging for tin-stone near the surface, mine-shafts were dug in many areas for better access to the tin and other minerals. Power was needed, and with the aid of leats and launders water was harnessed to turn the great water wheels that worked the crushers and the bellows that kept the smelting pits at the required heat. The survey map shows many places where the remains of industries can be found, and there are as many again that are unmarked. The routes of long dried up leats can be followed, usually ending in a jumble of fallen stones and the indentation of a pit; the remains of a blowing house that once employed many men all week.

Of course there was no transport for these men to go home every night, so from Monday to Saturday they lived on the moor, and working men must be housed and fed. Not that their huts would have done much to prosper the quarrying industry. Many were not much better than the hut circles that

It is difficult to imagine what Dartmoor must have looked like before man began to industrialise the area....

their Bronze age forefathers had lived in, but some of the larger mines had quite respectable quarters for their men.

Much of their food would have been brought up each week from their homes in places like Tavistock, Ashburton or Plymouth. Bread, meal for porridge, etc. would have kept for the week, but fresh meat was a problem – but this was where another Dartmoor industry came in very useful. Since Norman times, when the rabbit had been introduced to the British Isles, rabbits had formed a valuable supplement to the diet, especially in winter, when most of the stock was killed and salted down to overcome the lack of fodder. A nice fresh rabbit must have seemed a real treat to miner and town dweller alike, and so the warrening industry was formed, an industry which was to continue into this century.

The warren houses can still be seen, some have fallen into ruins, but some are still lived in. Radiating out from each warren house are the long humps of the warrens themselves, built of heaps of stone and turf covered. The rabbits lived and bred in comparative safety, made even more secure by the fact that the warreners built vermin traps in which to catch the weasels and stoats that would otherwise have attacked the rabbits in their warrens. When rabbits were required, their holes were netted, and they were caught with the aid of dogs. It is well worth a look at the fields close to the warren house, one of them will be seen to have square niches built into the thickness of the walls, this would have been the kennel field where the dogs were kept.

Rabbits were so important to the tinners that their emblem became the "Tinners Rabbit", three rabbits having two ears each, but only three ears between them as they are shown running in a continuous circle. These rabbits are depicted on the sign of the Warren House Inn, and may also be seen in a carving at Widecombe Church.

The rabbits were not kept solely for the miners, but would also have been carried by packhorse to feed the inhabitants of Plymouth and other large towns. Nor were the leats built just to serve the tin mines. As early as Elizabethan times a leat was dug to supply water for Plymouth, this was Drake's leat, a project organised by Drake when he was mayor of Plymouth.

Some of the Dartmoor Industry Stamps.

The peat cutting industry is probably thousands of years old. One can imagine the Bronze Age settlers sitting around a peat fire in their circular huts. The conical roof may have had a hole in the centre for the smoke to escape, but more likely the smoke just found its way out through any chinks it could find in the thatch. Many residents of Dartmoor and its surrounding villages still have rights of "turbary", i.e. peat cutting, today, though few take advantage of it; and peat cutting is fast becoming a dying skill, with the peat cutters tools being used as decorations for pub walls.

But as mentioned, peat was not only used as a domestic fuel. A vast amount was used in the smelting of tin, and at Shipley Bridge are the remains of a naptha works, where an unprofitable attempt was made to turn peat into naptha gas.

The carting of large amounts of peat to the works brought another offshoot to the list of Dartmoor industries. In order to get the peat from the centre of the moor down to Shipley Bridge, a railway was built. This was only one of the many that have been in use on the moor, and around the turn of the century the moor must have been almost an area of high density industry, and certainly provided employment for a good many people. In the centre of the South Moor, at Red Lake, there was a large clay works, involving another railway down to what is now the Western Machinery works at Bittaford. While the granite quarry at Haytor had its own granite tracked railway to carry stone to the Stover Canal, from which it travelled by boat to London and elsewhere.

Several books have been written about the industries of Dartmoor, so I will only mention two more enterprising ventures that were tried, and failed, both on the north moor. One was the ice works near Sourton Common, and the other was the glass works associated with Meldon Quarry.

Though there are signs of old industries all over Dartmoor, only two major industries are active today. There are still one or two quarries in operation, and the vast china clay works at Lee Moor looks like being with us for many years to come. But though most of the industries have died out, they are nearly all remembered, and marked, by letterboxes.

The mines have featured in many stamps, and some of the

The Aqueduct, a spectacular part of the Devonport Leat.

mines that have, or have had, letterboxes are: Hen Roost, Golden Dagger, Hooten Wheals, Wheal Jewel, Wheal Emma, Gibby Beam, T-Girt, London Pit and Wheal Katherine. The Glass Works and Ice Works each have had their letterbox. China Clay has had boxes at Crownhill Down, Left Lake and Red Lake, and the charcoal burning industry was remembered by a box at the "Meiler" on Wild Tor Ridge.

The Warreners are not forgotten. There are stamps at Huntingdon Warren, Willings Walls Warren and Trolsworthy, while "the Warreners of Dartymoor" moves from warren to warren. Warreners and Tinners have been united in one stamp, the Tinners Rabbit, which was at Ditsworthy Warren. Another unusual industry which merited its own box and stamp was the Gunpowder Mills, just north of the Twobridges to Postbridge road. The stamp showed the cannon used for testing the powder made on the site.

The peatcutters have been remembered at Eastern Red Lake, and Turf House below Lynch Tor. The railways nearly all have, or have had their boxes and stamps, from the earliest horse-drawn tramways, to the steam railway that crossed the moor from Yelverton to Princetown. Letterboxes come and go, but the remains of the old industries have now become an integral part of the fabric of Dartmoor, and more people have now become interested in the industrial archaeology of the moor through letterboxing, than for many other reasons. Not only has boxhunting sparked off an interest in man's remains, but in the legends of the moor, and in the wildlife. A great many people who took up letterboxing as a game now know a lot more about Dartmoor and its history.

For those who are interested in further reading on the history, legends and wildlife of the moor, there are many publications on sale. Most of these can be obtained from the Dartmoor National Park Authority centre at Parke, in Bovey Tracey, or from any of their information centres. These are placed at strategic sites on the moor – eg. Princetown and Postbridge, and are manned by people with a wide knowledge of the moor.

ERME PITS
DARTYMOOR
1980

HOOTEN
WHEALS
Est. 1979
DARTMOOR

DEVON MINES
1811

EYLESBARROW
TIN MINES

Dartmoor's Industry

MINES AND WORKINGS
OF THE PAST

GIBBY
BEAM

THE HAPPY MINER

Wheal Jewell
REDDAFORD LEAT
NORTH DARTMOOR

Stamps of some of Dartmoor's Mines.

Chapter 11

To the unobservant, Dartmoor can appear to be a rather dull wilderness of peat and bracken – with the ponies, sheep and cattle the only inhabitants. If you never go more than 100 yards from your car, this is the only animal life you are likely to see. But the serious walker (or letterboxer), who keeps his eyes open while walking in the centre of the south or north moor may well come across a variety of creatures, varying according to the time of year.

To start with the birds. Dartmoor is one of the few places in England where the raven is common, and in the area round Beardown Tors as many as 25 have been seen at one time. Buzzards, rooks and carrion crows are common, and in sheltered areas such as the head of the Erme Valley, where sheep tend to go to lamb, and in some cases to die, a crows' nest and a fox's earth can usually be found nearby – nature being a great opportunist. Kestrels and tawny owls are also plentiful, though it is not very likely that an owl will be spotted as one walks, but after dark they range widely over the open moorland. Herons too come surprisingly far up rivers, and may often be seen fishing in a stream that would seem too shallow for anything larger than a shrimp. Nearly all the other birds of prey that inhabit or visit the British Isles can be seen on occasions over Dartmoor. Even the osprey follows the Dart on its journey north; and one may be lucky enough to see a merlin, hobby, Montague's or hen harrier at most times of the year – and not always in the centre of the moor either, I have seen a hen harrier sitting majestically on a rock at the side of the road!

Cuckoo Rock.

Cuckoos are surprisingly common on Dartmoor. I have never been to the letterbox at Cuckoo Rock in the spring, without hearing at least one calling. We have been lucky enough to watch two "cuckoo incidents" on the moor, that I have not witnessed anywhere else. One was a young cuckoo, fully fledged, and to all appearances quite old enough to fend for itself, beseching its minute foster-parent, a meadow pipit, for food. The little bird, who had obviously twigged that she had been bamboozled, was trying to ignore the vast gaping beak, as her enormous baby followed her from post to post down a line of fencing. The other incident was the courtship of a pair of cuckoos. The calling and display of the male attracted another male who also displayed. We were so fascinated with watching the three birds, that box-hunting ground to a halt, while bird watching took over.

Red grouse can often be seen on the north moor, though not so often on the south. Black grouse, or blackcock are rarer. Golden plover and lapwings are present in large flocks in winter, as are fieldfare and redwing. Two of the more interesting smaller birds to be found on the moor are the ring-ouzel, which can sometimes be seen near old mine workings, and the dipper which can be found in, around or under the water of most of Dartmoor's fast flowing rivers.

There are an abundance of even smaller birds. One has only to stand still and listen to realise that there are larks everywhere in the summer, and often there seems to be a wheatear on every boulder. The wheatear is not, as one might think, a bird that lives in cultivated areas, but a summer inhabitant of heath and moorland. I have been told that its original common name was "white-arse", but that our more prudish Victorian ancestors could not bring themselves to use such a name, and so changed it. I cannot vouch for the truth of that story, but I must say, white-arse seems a logical name for a bird with such a conspicuous white rump.

Many of these Dartmoor birds are depicted on letterbox stamps – past or present, and other boxes are sited at places having names connected with birds.

Although Dartmoor does not abound in ducks, the oldest "bird" letterbox was the Crossing Memorial one at Duck's

A few of the Birds of Dartmoor.

Pool. The next oldest is the box at Cuckoo Rock. Unfortunately, probably because this box is very well known and is fairly close to the road, this very nice stamp has been stolen several times, and the box is continually being vandalised, to the great regret of all dedicated walkers.

As already mentioned, the very first home cut rubber stamp was of a bird. The mythical "Dartmoor warbler", sited at Smallbrook Head. Since then many birds have appeared, some only birds of passage as the stamps were only out for a short time. "Cuckoo in the Nest" might also be called a bird of passage, but that one is still travelling, and may pop up anywhere – regardless of the time of year!

Place names that have, or have had, bird stamps depicting their own particular bird are Crow Tor, Eagle Rock, Thrushel Combe, Hawks Tor, Crane Lake and Woodcock Hill. But birds have been used on many other stamps. The 1983 stamp at Belstone had a buzzard on, Leather Tor stamp is called the Cry of the Buzzard, Sandy Hole Pass is guarded by an owl, Black Tor has the Raven's Perch and "wild Dartmoor" at Wittabarrow had a picture of a hobby.

One of the legends of Dartmoor is that Chaw Gully Mine is protected by a raven, so the stamp there has a picture of a raven and the words "Guardian of Chaw Gully". There is even a letterbox on Sittaford Tor, put out by a German visitor, depicting a Habicht, (or in English, a goshawk).

...Vixen Tor, a remarkable pile of rock...

Chapter 12

Although the four legged fauna of Dartmoor appears on more stamps than the birds of Dartmoor do, it is scarcer and more rarely seen. There are, on average, four foxes to the square mile on Dartmoor, but it is unusual to come upon more than one in a day's walking. This is not entirely due to the fact that foxes are largely nocturnal, because for the greater part of the year foxes will sleep above ground, but one has to pass really close before they will disturb their rest and make a run across open country, before disappearing again into the gorse or clitter.

Fox Tor and Fox Tor Mires are well named, one can often come upon a fox in this area. The Fox Tor letterbox is one of the original few, and has a stamp of a running fox in it. Although this box has been vandalised several times since it was put out in 1975, the stamp has been replaced. There was also a box at Fox Tor Mires, though one is advised to walk with caution in this area, but there is a bridle-path marked through the mire, so in most weathers it is possible to get from one side to the other with dry feet.

Vixen Tor also has a letterbox, and though I am sure it was thus named because of foxes in the area, I personally have never seen one there. (Nor for that matter have I ever come upon Vixana, the witch who haunts the Tor.) The actual Tor is walled round, and is on private ground, though there is a stile on the side furthest from the road, where one can climb over and study the Tor – a remarkable pile of rock. But because the land is private the box is sited outside the wall.

Foxholes is another letterbox with a "foxy" stamp, and there are other stamps with foxes on at the Fox's Lair at Cosdon and at Brim Brook.

A Selection of Dartmoor Wildlife Stamps

Since the advent of myxamatosis, the rabbit population on Dartmoor has fluctuated, but at least it has had no effect on the number of rabbit stamps in the letterboxes. Of course the Warrens are obvious sites for a rabbit stamp, there is one at Willings Walls Warren, Huntingdon Warren and Ditsworthy Warren. The Tinners' Rabbits are on the stamp at Meldon Hill, and the common Dartmoor bunny is pictured on the stamp of "Beautiful Dartmoor". Nor are their adversaries the stoats and weasels forgotten, there is a Vermin Trap letterbox, and there are stoat stamps at Rue Lake Pit and the Valley of the Erme.

The badger, usually a creature of woodland, is surprisingly common on Dartmoor. Not that you are likely to see one when letterboxing, (unless you walk by night), but there are many active setts on the south moor. Badger watching is a compulsive hobby, and if you sit down-wind of an active colony at dusk on a May evening, you will probably be rewarded by seeing – first the cubs coming out to play, then the adults, emerging from the sett and having a good scratch, before they set out on their night's foraging. The badger has been depicted on the 1982 Belstone stamp, and the stamps at Vergyland Combe and at Ugborough Rocks.

Hare Tor, Hen Tor, Hound Tor and Hart Tor, though not really part of the fauna of the moor, have all lent their names and their pictures to letterboxes; and the otter, a rare sight on Dartmoor these days, has a box at Otter Pool. The mink, which has helped oust the otter from many of Devon's rivers, has not yet appeared on a stamp – but no doubt it is only a matter of time! The mink in fact are getting so bold that we have had to stop the car while one dragged a rabbit, larger than itself, across the road in front of us.

While talking of the creatures of the moor, one must not forget the adder. A creature which many look on with horror and suspicion. On the whole, one's chances of being bitten by an adder are very slight, and one's chances of even seeing one are small. In spite of this, I feel it is wise if small children wear wellingtons, and dogs are kept on leads in known adder areas in summer. I work on the principle that it is better to be safe than sorry, my niece was once bitten by one, and wasted

Stamps from some of the Warren Letterboxes.

three days of her Devon holiday in hospital! They are fairly localised, liking to bask on sunny boulder strewn slopes, or near bracken, but if they hear you coming, they will most likely slither off out of sight.

The 1981 Belstone stamp had an adder on it, Belstone Tor being in an adder area, and another box was actually guarded by an adder. This box was under a large boulder which happened to be the adder's home, and several times he (or she) was seen sunning himself by his front door. It is worth remembering to carry a stick when letterboxing in spring or summer, it can be most useful to prod under stones and clumps of heather with, when searching for an elusive box, you never know – the hole just *might* be occupied!

Bees abound on Dartmoor, and are not forgotten in the letterboxes either. There are "bee" stamps on Stingers Hill and Little Bee Tor, and the 1983 Honeybag Tor stamp is of a comb of honey surrounded by bees. There is also a charming dragon-fly stamp for the Brook Wanderer, which flits about like the dragon-fly it depicts. Perhaps one of the funniest, though hardly the most accurate of clues sent around was – "a Lepidopterist Supper" – the box was hidden at Woolholes.

The flora of the moors has so far been somewhat neglected by the stamp designers, though there has been a Bog Cotton stamp on the north moor, and a Whortleberry stamp at Hart Tor Brook. This still leaves the field wide open for a series of floral stamps. Sundews, though somewhat insignificant are to be found in lots of boggy places on the moor, three types of heather are abundant there, and orchids are to be found if you know where to look. The gorse provides striking patches of colour in the spring and autumn, and there are many flowers, common to the moors, which grow in few other places in the British Isles.

The Reverend William Keeble Martin made many of his meticulous drawings for the Concise British Flora on Dartmoor. In fact, he and his brother spent so many weekends on Dartmoor, in the period when their father was Rector of Dartington, that they built a small chapel on the moor for their Sunday worship. The remains of this, near Huntingdon Warren can still be seen today.

The Series of Stamps from the Belstone Box.

Chapter 13

As mentioned before, a correspondent to the Western Morning News compared letterboxing to skateboarding ie. a passing fad. Well, it is rare to see a skateboard these days, but the letterboxes are going strong! When that letter was written in 1979 there were about 40 boxes out, now there averages about 450 at a time – scattered over the moor. There have been to date, about 1,000 different boxes, but of course, some boxes are only intended to be out for a short time. Some indeed have a very short life. There was one with a stamp of a woodcock in, and after it had been found, the next caller to the site found no stamp, no visitors book – just a note – "The Woodcock has been shot"! Others have a longer life than this, but obviously no one wants to collect a stamp commemorating say the Queen's Jubilee, or the Royal Wedding, a year after the event.

A new aspect to letterboxing was started by the Dartmoor Youth Training Centre, near Prince Hall. There the letterbox is not hidden, but is in an outhouse, and all callers may sign the visitors book and collect a print of the stamp without having to tramp for miles. This idea next spread to the Plume of Feathers Inn at Princetown, a pub much used by walkers. The visitors book is always a good place to find out any information about new boxes. In fact they are now on their second visitors book, and the first one has been given to the Plymouth Museum.

The Museum of Dartmoor Life at Okehampton has joined in on this new style of letterbox, and among the relics of Dartmoor's ancient industries, are the necessities for one of Dartmoor's newer industries, a little chest containing visitors

The Plume of Feathers Inn at Princetown, a pub much used by walkers...

book, stamp and ink-pad, in other words – a Dartmoor Letterbox.

There can not be many who do not already know about the Dartmoor Letterboxes – if the variety of addresses that appear in the visitors books are anything to go by. A dip into an old Honeybag Tor book shows visitors from Bromsgrove, Southampton, Axminster, Hampton in Middlesex, Bristol, Holland and Germany, all on the first few pages. To say nothing of all the Devonians of course.

There seems to be as much of a national element about those who own letterboxes too. Looking through the "official" box caretakers, one finds the Boys Brigade from Crawley, who put out a box at Bala Brook to commemorate their centenary. The Outdoor Activities Group from H.M. Borstal at Guys Marsh have put out a box in memory of Philip Guy Stevens. The Apprentices from Leyland Cars Swindon had a box at Watern Tor commemorating their Duke of Edinburgh Awards.

Other official bodies, or groups of people owning boxes are:– Rangers from Dartmouth. Exeter University and the Western Morning News, who jointly own the Flat Tor box. The 21st. Plymouth Scouts, who put out the Fish Lake box in 1968. The 4th. Teignmouth Scouts, who discovered Grant's Pot, a small underground cavern, in 1953, intended to put out a letterbox there but failed to do so. However a box was set up at this site in 1972 by the pupils of Dawlish Secondary School. The Fur Tor box was put out by the Junior Leaders Regiment in 1951. The "Moorland Rambler", a shop catering for walkers climbers and campers, has a box at Kit Rocks – perhaps a pun on the fact that they supply kit! And the Exeter Round About Club (whoever they may be) also own a box.

A few boxes are placed as memorials. Of course the first of these was the Duck's Pool box, in memory of William Crossing, but many of them have a purely personal aspect. Bellever Tor had a box in memory of "Linda, who loved this area". Shell Top box was in memory of Ella Manley – 1888–1978. Black Tor has a box in memory of "My Brother Brent", who was sadly killed in a motor bike accident. Animals too

Stamps Commemorating People and Events (and a cat).

are not forgotten, Tinkers Bridge box is in memory of "Tinker", a cat, and Blue Monty, a Dartmoor Prison guard dog had a box in his honour.

I can think of few lovelier places to be remembered than on Dartmoor, with its serene landscapes and rugged Tors. It is nice to think that as well as the sadder ghosts of Benjie, Childe and Jay, whose little grave lies at the roadside north of Hound Tor. There may be many happier wanderers from the next life returning to recapture pleasant hours spent on the moor.

Chapter 14

Letterboxing is not a select club, where clues and advice are only given to the chosen few. There are probably several thousand boxhunters to date – with more joining the ranks every day. The main reasons for the element of secrecy about the whereabouts of most of the boxes are:–

(1) If boxes were not hidden well, the moor might appear to have developed a rash of ice-cream cartons and ammunition boxes, which would not only look very untidy but would completely revoke the carefully thought out "Code of Conduct". (2) Even the nicest of places is not safe from vandals, and as a professionally made stamp costs about £12, no one wants to get their stamp stolen within the first few weeks of putting it out. And (3) the whole idea of the original box at Cranmere Poolwas that to reach it was a challenge, the idea of a challenge still exists. Not so much perhaps in walking to the site, as was the case at Cranmere Pool, but in working out clues, following compass bearings, reading maps, and in many cases, knowing the stories and legends of Dartmoor.

Though the Park Authorities have no part in letterboxing, they do forward queries from novices who have heard about the presence of boxes on the moor, but have no idea of how to go about looking for them. Though in these days of expensive postage it is only courteous to enclose an extra stamp if they are expected to send a letter on. Plymouth Library not only holds the old visitors books from the Cranmere Pool box, but also has a few other items on letterboxes in the reference section.

The equipment used for boxhunting varies from minimal to as extravagent as you care to make it. But when it comes to clothes, it is as well to remember that Dartmoor can be a place of many moods. Most serious walkers favour walking boots, the going can be very rough, and a day's walking will very likely take you over an assorted terrain. This may well vary from the short, close nibbled grass, which can be very slippery, areas of gorse and heather where it is difficult to see where you are putting your feet, patches of bog, and the clitter strewn side of a tor. So strong footwear is essential.

Having said that, I have never possessed a pair of walking boots in my life! I prefer to walk in wellingtons. The men's sort, because they have a much better cleated sole which gives them a better grip on most types of ground, and also leaves room for thick socks, which gives them a much firmer grip round the ankles. But I must confess that I spend a lot of my working day in "wellies", so they are what my feet are used to. They are not everyone's cup of tea, and are frowned on by many. Training shoes can be worn in summer – IF you have good strong ankles, and IF they have good rubber soles, but, be warned, plastic soles can feel like roller skates on short dry turf. The simple answer is that, as for any sort of walking, footwear should be strong, sound and comfortable.

Roughly speaking, clothes should be the same. As letterbox hunters vary from the holiday-maker who is only looking for the odd box or two, on an afternoon's stroll, half a mile from his car – to the dedicated boxhunter, who will walk from dawn to dusk, all year and in all weathers, – clothes must suit the occasion.

Anyone walking on Dartmoor, (by that, I mean anyone going more than a mile from their car), should always have more clothes than they think they need. Even on a summer's day the mist can come from nowhere, and within minutes the temperature will drop 10 degrees, or a passing cloud can bring an icy shower, it may only last five minutes – but can leave one soaked. A lightweight cagoule and a scarf or woolly

One of Dartmoor's Potato Caves, used as a letterbox site.

hat can make all the difference between misery and an enjoyable summer walk. Add a map, an apple and a bar of chocolate in your pocket and you are ready for a little light letterboxing.

As you progress and go further into the centre of the moor, so should your equipment progress. At this stage, a rucksack becomes necessary. The average walking speed on the moor is two miles an hour, add to this some extra time for looking for boxes, or just enjoying the scenery, and you will find you are wanting to carry your lunch with you and make a day of it. Do not forget that a hot drink or some soup will be most welcome in winter, and walking can be thirsty work in summer. Dartmoor streams look inviting and crystal clear, but there may well be a *very* dead sheep in the water higher up, so – you have been warned – take plenty to drink in hot weather, especially when walking with children.

While on the subject of children, boxhunting can be a great incentive to younger members of the family who might find walking for walking's sake a dull proposition. A group of young boys from a certain school who are regular boxhunters enjoy "action packed weekends", (their phrase, not mine). Boxhunters come in all ages, the youngest as previously mentioned is four months, and the oldest regular that I know of is in his 70's, though there may well be older – or younger.

The next most important requirement is a compass. Not only may a Dartmoor mist leave you with a visibility of only 25 yards, but you may well find you are given a compass bearing as a guide to an elusive box. So you would be well advised to carry a compass – and make sure you know how to use it!

A good map is important. The Ordnance Survey Tourist map of Dartmoor is a good one to start with. Rights of way, objects of Archaeological interest, the Army Firing Ranges and guides as to the terrain are all clearly marked. Later you may want to progress to the 1:25,000 (or two and a half inches to the mile), but these come in small sections and are fairly pricey, so they can be added gradually to your collection.

While on the subject of Firing Ranges, days in which firing is to take place on any particular range are advertised in the

All that remains of Huntingdon Warren Farmhouse.

"Western Morning News", "Express and Echo" and the "Western Times and Gazette" every Friday, and can also be seen in local Police Stations, Post Offices and certain Inns. There is no firing on the moor in the month of August. One must be careful not to touch any strange object found in any of these areas, but to report any such find to a local Police Station.

While it is much safer to walk in the middle of Dartmoor than to cross the road, it is as well to remember a few simple precautions. If you are walking on your own, you should always tell someone, beforehand, where you are intending to go. Anyone can twist an ankle and find themselves incapable of getting off the moor, but if someone knows in what area to look for you, you will save everyone a lot of time and trouble. A wise walker will be supplied with, at the very least, a bar of chocolate or Kendal Mint Cake and some form of extra clothing, which should include one brightly coloured item so that they can be easily spotted. A whistle can be very useful in fog, and a torch can come in handy if walking late in winter.

Though Dartmoor may seem to be covered with hazards such as mine shafts and bogs, you are extremely unlikely to come to grief in any of these, if in doubt stick to pony and sheep tracks – if they can walk with safety, so can you. Just remember not to go rushing about in a fog, or you may end up with wet feet. Use your map and compass and watch where you are putting your feet, probably more accidents happen from people just tripping over than from all other hazards put together!

Now you have the basic equipment to take you anywhere on Dartmoor, you will gradually add more letterboxing gear. Someone may have pinched the pen out of the box you are going to, so a pen is useful. The ink-pad in the box may have run out, so your own ink-pad is an idea. What are you collecting your stamps on? Take some paper or postcards with you. If you want a really good impression of the stamp, you need a hard surface to press on, pop a small square of plywood in your rucksack, and your stamping will be much easier. Few rucksacks keep out every drop of wet, so how

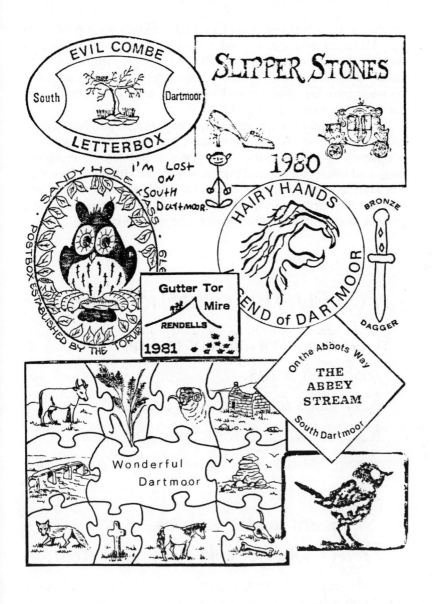

Dartmoor Letterbox Stamps (3) including the original bird rubber cut.

about a few polythene bags in which to keep your postcards etc? How do you get a good impression of a stamp in wet weather? Some carry an umbrella or large polythene sheet to stamp up under. You probably have a few ideas of your own so now you can understand why the dedicated letterboxer carries such a large rucksack!

Of course when we started this chapter, we just had a map and an apple in our pockets, and you may never want to progress beyond this stage, but – be warned, letterboxing is a bug, and once you catch it you may well be bitten for life. You can start at any age, and continue as long as you can put one foot in front of the other, so think carefully before you collect your first stamp, and after that: Happy Letterboxing.

FOLLOW THE COUNTRY CODE

Guard against all risk of fire.

Fasten all gates.

Keep dogs under proper control.

Keep to paths across farmland.

Avoid damaging fences, hedges and walls.

Leave no litter.

Safeguard water supplies.

Protect wildlife, wild plants and trees.

Chapter 15

"Well I never!
Did you ever
Hear of such a hooter!
Boxes (letter)
Bigger, better,
Shoved through a computer!

For a fiver
Will arrive a
Print-out situation.
Mr. Swinscow:
Will you please now
Take my application."

Yes, I suppose it was only a matter of time before modern science caught up with the listing of letterboxes. And though Sylvia Tancock's request for a list is the only one (so far) received in rhyme, it is certainly not the only request received.

To ensure that a list of the current 450 or so boxes does not fall into the hands of some vandal who might destroy them, or have a fancy to tip 450 visitors books and 450 rubber stamps into Drake's Leat, the print-out list of boxes is only available to those who are members of the 100 club. Working on the principle that if anyone has been already keen enough to collect 100 different boxes, they are not likely to destroy or damage the rest.

At the moment the print-out is a limited edition, and is still in its infancy, so whether it will continue in its present form, take some different form, or fade out, is a matter that only time will sort out, but as most keen boxhunters kept a list in some form or another, it seems logical that there should be a common list.

Technology catches up with most things, and computerised lists are not the only new things on the moor. Several walkers now carry C.B. radio. Thus boxhunters can now communicate with each other over greater distances than before, and messages such as "Diptford Hound calling Moorover, I've found the box 300 yards below the Tor, 5 paces from a lone rowan tree – will wait there for you." Or perhaps just "I've had enough, will meet you back at the car", can now be relayed across a stretch of moor that would take an hour to walk.

Luckily these are modern inventions that in no way disturb the peace of the moor, and one model areoplane can make more of a disturbance than 500 letterboxers! Luckily there are 365 square miles of Dartmoor, so there should be space for everyone to carry out their pursuits without upsetting others. Especially as the vast percentage of visitors to the moor go no further than 100 yards from their cars, and ask for no more than to sit in a deck chair admiring the view and eating ice-creams. Everyone to their choice.

The same applies to letterboxing, if you are a fanatic who needs a computerised list and a C.B. radio, good luck to you. But if you enjoy a beautiful walk with a bit of a challenge, then good luck to you too.

You may walk 5 miles only to find that the box you were after has been taken in, or re-sited somewhere else, or you may meet another letterboxer who tells of 2 new boxes with lovely stamps, right on your route. It's all in a day's luck.

Boxer's Lament

"GOD DAMN IT, it's gone!" re-echoes the cry;
Ringing up from the moor to an unconcerned sky.
The sheep scatter wildly, more placid cows graze;
at the solitary figure in silent amaze.
He's raging and stamping, he's broken his stick;
One gathers his feelings are cut to the quick.
His rucksack he's hurled to the ground in a rage.
His language 'mongst ladies would surely outrage.
The obvious results of this violent emotion,
are regrettably adding to Dartmoor's erosion.
The black granite tors standing grim and aloof;
glower down on the scene with inherent reproof.
Brock badger below in his moist earthy den,
casts a look at his roof 'lest it fall in again.

A vixen nearby with an earth of young foxes
says "It's something to do with the humans and boxes,
Some hide 'em, some find 'em, some take 'em away
but whether they like it I really can't say."
The "human" meanwhile with emotion profound
In anguish has thrown himself down on the ground
A typical "boxer" in gaiters and shirt,
His hands smeared with ink-stains and peat burns and
dirt.
Sun tanned and sweaty, mud up to his knees;
Used to hard walking not bothered with ease.
He looks wild and grim, there's a snarl on his face;
What could have upset him in this lonely place?
He stands by a hole that's concealed by a rock,
and it seems to have something to do with his shock.
He clutches a bag with a message therein
A small piece of card with the words – "TAKEN IN".

It has happened to most of us, but "El Hombre" has
expressed the feeling for us all, however – it is *ONLY* A
GAME".

Stop Press

Since Dartmoor Letterboxes first appeared in print, many boxes have come and gone on the moor, till now in 1987 there are about 1,000. Before you start to think that there cannot be 1,000 hiding places on the moor, I will explain that a great number are in pubs or in letterboxer's rucksacks.

As mentioned in Chapter 13, the Plume of Feathers Inn at Princetown has a letterbox. This was the original idea of the landlord and his friends, themselves letterboxers, and as the pub is situated in the middle of the moor, a little "pub letterboxing" can make a welcome break to an expedition. Other pubs soon caught on to the idea that a letterbox behind the bar could bring in extra trade, and now a lot of pubs and a few cafes have their own stamp and visitors book, all attractive and collectable, though not the kind of letterboxing that qualifies one for membership of the "100 Club"! They do have one great advantage though, many people write news of new boxes in the back of visitors books, and it is very pleasant to be able to get some up to date information in comfort, over a cup of tea or a pint and a pasty.

The boxes that are hidden in walkers' rucksacks are known as "Travellers", and again – though not true letterboxing – they can provide a lot of fun and provide a very good way for letterboxers to meet others with the same hobby. All one needs is a nice stamp (preferably with a Dartmoor connection) and a visitors' book and you are away, you have a travelling box. As you walk over the moor in search of more traditional boxes, don't be suprised if total strangers approach you and say "Excuse me, but have you a Traveller?" it can be a very good way of making friends, and provides an added interest for young and possibly slightly reluctant walkers.

So many people are now interested in letterboxing that the twice yearly get-together or "meet" of walkers and letterboxers has outgrown the Forest Inn, and for the past two "clock change" days the venue has been moved to the Prison Officers Club at Princetown. Also, with the large number of boxes and boxers, the computer catalogue of boxes has been continued – at least for the time being. Several people circulate lists of "up-dates", and as some boxes are only out for a short time this is probably the best method. For anyone completely new to letterboxing, I should advise them to start with those boxes that are shown on the Ordnance Survey map – especially Cranmere Pool, the ancestor of all letterboxes.

Since James Perrot, the Dartmoor guide, first hid a jar in a bank at Cranmere Pool, letterboxing has come a long way. The respectable Victorian ladies and gentlemen who braved the elements to reach the pool may seem far removed from the letterboxer of today, but they have two things in common:– the enjoyment of a challenge and a love of Dartmoor.

Sooner or later, everyone who walks on Dartmoor comes under its spell, it is impossible to be out hunting for hidden boxes without noticing the beauty and grandeur about you. To quote from a poem by "Noddy" about a Spring walk across the moor:–

> ....I came to a tor and clambered up
> To view the landscape from the top,
> Beauty spread for miles before me,
> Dartmoor's treasure in all its glory.
>
> Distant tors stand proud and still,
> Majestic crowns that grace the hills,
> Granite Gods, each one unique,
> Shaped by time from foot to peak....

Our National Parks are a heritage we must preserve, look after and enjoy.–

"Good Hunting"

CODES OF CONDUCT

Please be aware that:

Most of Dartmoor is privately owned.
Your rights on common land are only to walk or ride.
You walk elsewhere only by courtesy of the owners, except on rights of way.
... these rights and privileges must not be abused, so show your appreciation
of the Dartmoor National Park and its landowners by ... adhering to the
letterbox Owners' and Hunters' Code of Conduct, and to the Country Code,
and educating others in this practice.

THE LETTERBOX OWNERS' CODE

Boxes should not be sited:

1. On land to which the public does not have access.
2. In any kind of antiquity, in or near stone rows or circles, cists or cairns. Nor
in any kind of building, walls or ruins, peat cutters' or tinners' huts etc.
3. In any potentially dangerous situation where injuries could be caused.
4. As a fixture. Cement or any other kind of building material is not to be used.
5. Other than in an existing natural hole or cavity, so that there is no
disturbance of rocks or vegetation — byelaws prohibit the cutting of turf.
6. Close to each other. Over-intensive use of an area causes damage to the
moorland surface.
7. Without a contact's phone number or address in the visitors' book.

THE LETTERBOX HUNTERS' CODE

1. When searching for boxes, do not disturb any antiquities such as stone rows,
circles, cists or cairns, nor any buildings, walls or ruins, peat cutters' or tinners'
huts etc.
2. It should never be necessary to remove natural vegetation or rocks to find
a box.
3. Replace the box carefully, and leave it as you would hope to find it.
4. Please help by taking away any litter left by people who care for the Moor
less than you do.
5. Dogs must be kept under proper control at all times. Under Park byelaws
a ranger can require a dog to be put on a lead, owners of dogs causing trouble
to sheep can be fined up to £400.
6. Follow the Country Code.